Step-by-Step
PROBLEM SOLVING

Grade 2

Thinking Kids®
Carson-Dellosa Publishing LLC
Greensboro, North Carolina

Credits

Content Editor: Christine Schwab
Copy Editor: Jesse Koziol
Layout and Cover Design: Lori Jackson

Visit carsondellosa.com for correlations to Common Core, state, national, and Canadian provincial standards.

Copyright © 2012, Singapore Asia Publishers Pte Ltd

Carson-Dellosa Publishing LLC
PO Box 35665
Greensboro, NC 27425 USA
carsondellosa.com

ISBN 978-1-60996-477-1
03-226171151

Introduction

The **Step-by-Step Problem Solving** series focuses on the underlying processes and strategies essential to problem solving. Each book introduces various skill sets and builds on them as the level increases. The six-book series covers the following thinking skills and heuristics:

Thinking Skills
- Analyzing Parts and Wholes
- Comparing
- Classifying
- Identifying Patterns and Relationships
- Deduction
- Induction
- Spatial Visualization

Heuristics
- Act It Out
- Draw a Diagram/Model
- Look for a Pattern
- Work Backward
- Make a List/Table
- Guess and Check
- Before and After
- Make Suppositions
- Use Equations

Students who are keen to develop their abilities in problem solving will learn quickly how to:
- make sense of the problem sum: what am I asked to find?
- make use of given information: what do I know?
- think of possible strategies: have I come across similar problems before?
- choose the correct strategy: apply what I know confidently.
- solve the problem: work out the steps.
- check the answer: is the solution logical and reasonable?

Practice questions follow each skill-set example, and three graded mixed practices (easy, intermediate, challenging) are provided for an overall assessment of the skills learned. The worked solutions show the application of the strategies used. Students will find this series invaluable in helping them understand and master problem-solving skills.

Table of Contents

Strategy Summary

The following summary provides examples of the various skill sets taught in Step-by-Step Problem Solving.

Page 6 Skill Set 1-A: Analyzing Parts and Wholes
Analyzing parts and wholes is a basic and useful way of looking at a problem. To analyze parts and wholes is to recognize the parts and understand how they form the whole.
Example: There are 5 apples and 6 oranges. How many pieces of fruit are there altogether?
Think
- Identify the parts: 5 apples and 6 oranges.
- Identify the whole: total number of pieces of fruit.
- Draw the part-whole model.
- Fill in the data to find the answer.
Solve

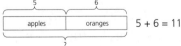

$5 + 6 = 11$

Answer There are **11 pieces of fruit** altogether.

Page 8 Skill Set 1-B: Analyzing Parts and Wholes
Sometimes, a problem tells us the whole but not the parts. Use the part-whole model to solve the problem.
Example: Logan has 18 markers. His friend borrows 6 markers from him. How many markers does Logan have left?

Think
- Identify the whole: 18 total markers.
- Identify the parts: 6 borrowed, ? left.
- Draw the part-whole model.
- Fill in the data to find the answer.
Solve

$18 - 6 = 12$

Answer Logan has **12 markers** left.

Page 10 Skill Set 1-C: Analyzing Parts and Wholes
Some problems can have multiple parts. You can still use the part-whole model to help you solve these problems.
Example: Jessica has a rock collection. She has 7 black rocks, 3 blue rocks, and 4 white rocks. How many rocks does Jessica have in her collection?
Think
- Identify the parts: 7 black rocks, 3 blue rocks, and 4 white rocks.
- Identify the whole: total number of rocks.
- Draw the part-whole model.
- Fill in the data to find the answer.

© Singapore Asia Publishers Pte Ltd • FS-704114

Strategy Summary

The following summary provides examples of the various skill sets taught in Step-by-Step Problem Solving.

Solve

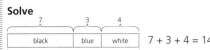

7 + 3 + 4 = 14

Answer   There are **14 rocks** in Jessica's collection.

Page 11 Skill Set 2-A: Comparing

Comparing is an effective way of identifying the relationship between the variables in a problem. Comparing the information in a problem helps us determine the differences in variables' quantities (for example, more or less).

Example: Jayla has 6 apples. Renee has 2 more apples than Jayla. How many apples does Renee have?

Think

• How many more apples does Renee have than Jayla?
• Draw the comparison model.
• Fill in the data to find the answer.

Solve

6 + 2 = 8

Answer   Renee has **8 apples**.

Page 13 Skill Set 2-B: Comparing

Sometimes, a problem involves subtraction instead of addition. Use the comparison model to solve the problem.

Example: There are 10 boys in a class. There are 3 fewer girls in the same class. How many girls are in the class?

Think

• How many fewer girls are there than boys?
• Draw the comparison model.
• Fill in the data to find the answer.

Solve

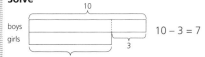

10 − 3 = 7

Answer   There are **7 girls** in the class.

Page 15 Skill Set 2-C: Comparing

Some problems can have multiple parts involving both addition and subtraction. We can still use the comparison model to help us solve these problems.

Example: Caleb has 9 fish. Drew has 3 more fish than Caleb. Ethan has 6 fewer fish than Drew. How many fish does Ethan have?

Think

• How many more fish does Drew have than Caleb?
• How many fewer fish does Ethan have than Drew?
• Draw the comparison model.
• Fill in the data to find the answer.

Solve

Caleb
Drew
Ethan

9 + 3 − 6 = 6

Answer   Ethan has **6 fish**.

Page 16 Skill Set 3-A: Act It Out

Act It Out is especially helpful when it is difficult to visualize a given problem. Act out the situation from the problem or use objects to represent the variables in the problem.

Example: There are 2 pairs of children: John and Tony, Mia and Sasha. Each boy needs to shake hands with each girl. How many handshakes are exchanged altogether?

Think

• Act it out! Get 4 friends (2 boys and 2 girls) to act out the story.

Solve

Answer   **4 handshakes** are exchanged altogether.

Page 19 Skill Set 3-B: Act It Out

Besides acting out a situation, we can sometimes use concrete items, such as toothpicks, to help solve a problem.

Example: The picture below is made up of 9 toothpicks. Remove 2 toothpicks so that the remaining toothpicks form 2 triangles.

Think

• We can either remove 2 toothpicks from the outside or 2 toothpicks from the inside.

Solve

   Remove 2 toothpicks from the inside.

Answer

Page 21 Skill Set 4-A: Draw a Diagram

Drawing a diagram is very useful because we can see the relationships and patterns among the data found in the problem. It is a good and effective way to organize the data.

Example: Mom has three packages: A, B, and C. Package A is heavier than package B but lighter than package C. Which package is the heaviest?

Think

• We know A is heavier than B but lighter than C.
• Draw a diagram to show this relationship.

Solve

Answer   **Package C** is the heaviest.

Analyzing parts and wholes is a basic and useful way of looking at a problem. To analyze parts and wholes is to recognize the parts and understand how they form the whole.

Example:
There are 5 apples and 6 oranges. How many pieces of fruit are there altogether?

 Think
- Identify the parts: 5 apples and 6 oranges.
- Identify the whole: total number of pieces of fruit.
- Draw the part-whole model.
- Fill in the data to find the answer.

 Solve

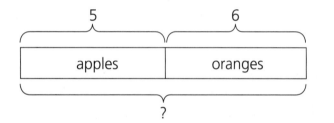

$$5 + 6 = 11$$

 Answer There are **11 pieces of fruit** altogether.

Give it a try!

There are 7 white bunnies and 3 brown bunnies. How many bunnies are there altogether?

 Think
Fill in the data to find the answer.

 Solve

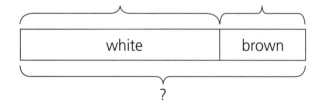

_____ + _____ = _____

 Answer There are _____ **bunnies** altogether.

(Answer: 10)

Practice: Analyzing Parts and Wholes

1. Tasha has 4 red beads and 8 blue beads. How many beads does she have altogether?

💡 **Think**

✏️ **Solve**

⭐ **Answer**

2. There are 10 cars in parking lot A and 12 cars in parking lot B. How many cars are there altogether?

💡 **Think**

✏️ **Solve**

⭐ **Answer**

Sometimes, a problem tells us the whole but not the parts. Use the part-whole model to solve the problem.

Example:
Logan has 18 markers. His friend borrows 6 markers from him. How many markers does Logan have left?

 Think
- Identify the whole: 18 total markers.
- Identify the parts: 6 borrowed, ? left.
- Draw the part-whole model.
- Fill in the data to find the answer.

 Solve

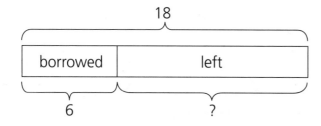

$18 - 6 = 12$

 Answer Logan has **12 markers** left.

Give it a try!

The produce market has 22 pears. If 11 of them are sold, how many pears are left?

 Think
Fill in the data to find the answer.

 Solve

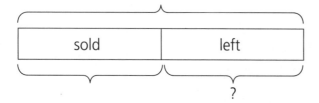

_____ – _____ = _____

Answer There are_____ **pears** left.

(Answer: 11)

Practice: Analyzing Parts and Wholes

3. There are 25 eggs in an egg tray. Jan breaks 8 of them. How many eggs are not broken?

💡 **Think**

✏️ **Solve**

⭐ **Answer**

4. Sally has 30 stickers in her album. She gives 14 of them to her brother. How many stickers does Sally have left?

💡 **Think**

✏️ **Solve**

⭐ **Answer**

Skill Set 1-C: Analyzing Parts and Wholes

Some problems can have multiple parts. You can still use the part-whole model to help you solve these problems.

Example:
Jessica has a rock collection. She has 7 black rocks, 3 blue rocks, and 4 white rocks. How many rocks does Jessica have in her collection?

 Think
- Identify the parts: 7 black rocks, 3 blue rocks, and 4 white rocks.
- Identify the whole: total number of rocks.
- Draw the part-whole model.
- Fill in the data to find the answer.

 Solve

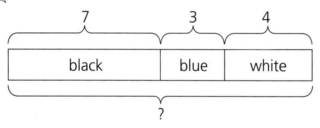

$7 + 3 + 4 = 14$

 Answer There are **14 rocks** in Jessica's collection.

Challenge yourself!

5. Alvin has a book. He reads 6 pages on Monday, 8 pages on Tuesday, and 5 pages on Wednesday. How many pages does he read altogether?

 Think

 Solve

 Answer

Skill Set 2-A: Comparing

Comparing is an effective way of identifying the relationship between the variables in a problem. Comparing the information in a problem helps us determine the differences in variables' quantities (for example, more or less).

Example:
Jayla has 6 apples. Renee has 2 more apples than Jayla. How many apples does Renee have?

 Think
- How many more apples does Renee have than Jayla?
- Draw the comparison model.
- Fill in the data to find the answer.

 Solve

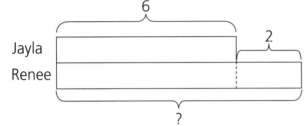

$6 + 2 = 8$

 Answer Renee has **8 apples**.

Give it a try!

Adam has 7 toy cars. Barry has 3 more toy cars than Adam. How many toy cars does Barry have?

 Think
Fill in the data to find the answer.

 Solve

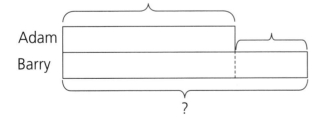

_____ + _____ = _____

 Answer Barry has _____ **toy cars**.

1. Daniel has 8 storybooks. He has 4 more comic books than storybooks. How many comic books does he have?

💡 **Think**

✏️ **Solve**

⭐ **Answer**

2. Mrs. Lee buys 10 roses. She buys 8 more carnations than roses. How many carnations does she buy?

💡 **Think**

✏️ **Solve**

⭐ **Answer**

Sometimes, a problem involves subtraction instead of addition. Use the comparison model to solve the problem.

Example:
There are 10 boys in a class. There are 3 fewer girls in the same class. How many girls are in the class?

 Think
- How many fewer girls are there than boys?
- Draw the comparison model.
- Fill in the data to find the answer.

 Solve

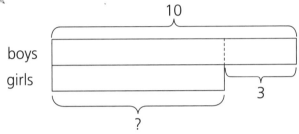

$10 - 3 = 7$

⭐ **Answer** There are **7 girls** in the class.

Give it a try!

Amy colors 13 roses red. She colors 6 fewer roses purple. How many roses does Amy color purple?

 Think
Fill in the data to find the answer.

 Solve

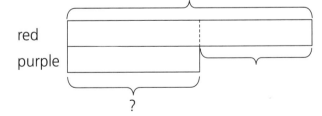

_____ − _____ = _____

⭐ **Answer** Amy colors _____ **roses** purple.

(Answer: 7)

3. Ronald takes 15 red balls from a basket. He takes 5 fewer blue balls than red balls from the same basket. How many blue balls does Ronald take?

💡 **Think**

✏️ **Solve**

⭐ **Answer**

4. Mrs. Howard sells 16 toasters. Mrs. Lewis sells 4 fewer toasters than Mrs. Howard. How many toasters does Mrs. Lewis sell?

💡 **Think**

✏️ **Solve**

⭐ **Answer**

Skill Set 2-C: Comparing

Some problems can have multiple parts involving both addition and subtraction. We can still use the comparison model to help us solve these problems.

Example:

Caleb has 9 fish. Drew has 3 more fish than Caleb. Ethan has 6 fewer fish than Drew. How many fish does Ethan have?

 Think

- How many more fish does Drew have than Caleb?
- How many fewer fish does Ethan have than Drew?
- Draw the comparison model.
- Fill in the data to find the answer.

 Solve

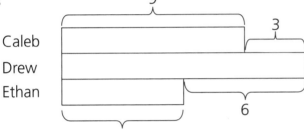

$$9 + 3 - 6 = 6$$

 Answer Ethan has **6 fish**.

Challenge yourself!

5. There are 12 cupcakes on tray A. There are 6 more cupcakes on tray B than on tray A. There are 4 fewer cupcakes on tray C than on tray B. How many cupcakes are on tray C?

 Think

 Solve

 Answer

Skill Set 3-A: Act It Out

Act It Out is especially helpful when it is difficult to visualize a given problem. Act out the situation from the problem or use objects to represent the variables in the problem.

Example:

There are 2 pairs of children: John and Tony, Mia and Sasha. Each boy needs to shake hands with each girl. How many handshakes are exchanged altogether?

 Think

• Act it out! Get 4 friends (2 boys and 2 girls) to act out the story.

 Solve

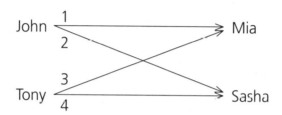

 Answer **4 handshakes** are exchanged altogether.

Give it a try!

Peter and Jan join the 2 pairs of children above. Again, each boy needs to shake hands with each girl. How many handshakes are exchanged altogether this time?

 Think

Act it out! Get 6 friends (3 boys and 3 girls) to act out the story.

 Solve

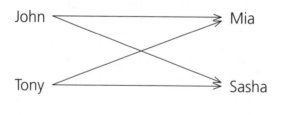

 Answer _____ **handshakes** are exchanged altogether.

(Answer: 9)

Practice: Act It Out

1. There are 3 boys on a sports team. Their coach wants to select 2 boys to be the team leaders. How many different pairs of leaders can the coach select?

💡 **Think**

✏️ **Solve**

⭐ **Answer**

2. Jerry has 3 T-shirts and 2 pairs of shorts. He has to match a T-shirt with a pair of shorts. In how many different ways can he match them?

💡 **Think**

✏️ **Solve**

⭐ **Answer**

3. Mackenzie has a pair of white shoes and a pair of black shoes. She also has 4 pairs of socks in 4 different colors. In how many ways can she pair her socks with her shoes?

 Think

Solve

⭐ **Answer**

Besides acting out a situation, we can sometimes use concrete items, such as toothpicks, to help solve a problem.

Example:
The picture below is made up of 9 toothpicks. Remove 2 toothpicks so that the remaining toothpicks form 2 triangles.

 Think
- We can either remove 2 toothpicks from the outside or 2 toothpicks from the inside.

 Solve

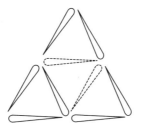

Remove 2 toothpicks from the inside.

 Answer

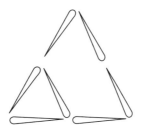

Practice: Act It Out

4. The picture below is made up of 12 toothpicks. Remove 2 toothpicks so that the remaining toothpicks form 2 squares.

💡 **Think**

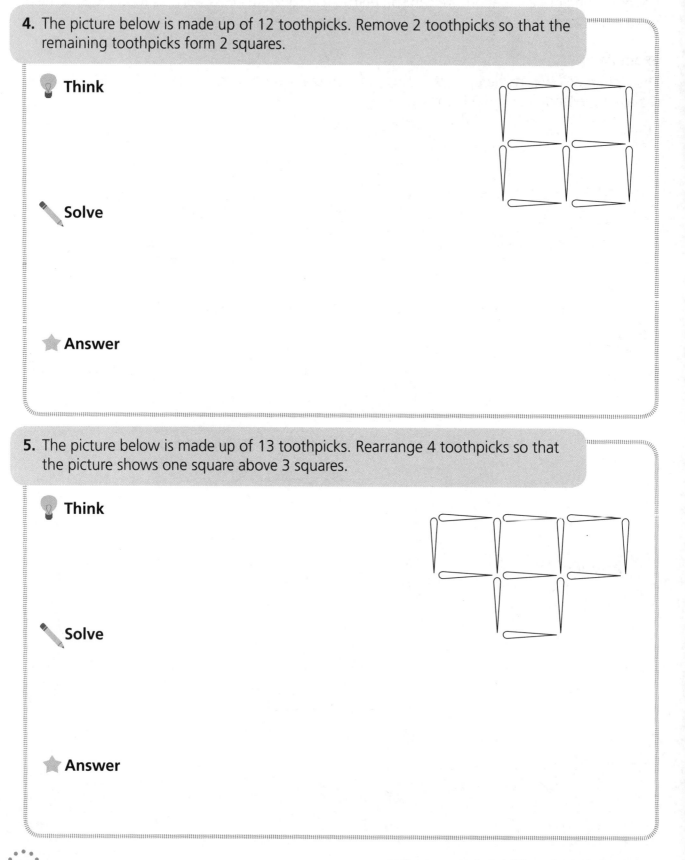

✏️ **Solve**

⭐ **Answer**

5. The picture below is made up of 13 toothpicks. Rearrange 4 toothpicks so that the picture shows one square above 3 squares.

💡 **Think**

✏️ **Solve**

⭐ **Answer**

Drawing a diagram is very useful because we can see the relationships and patterns among the data found in the problem. It is a good and effective way to organize the data.

Example:

Mom has three packages: A, B, and C. Package A is heavier than package B but lighter than package C. Which package is the heaviest?

 Think
- We know A is heavier than B but lighter than C.
- Draw a diagram to show this relationship.

Solve

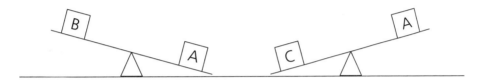

⭐ **Answer** **Package C** is the heaviest.

Give it a try!

Dad has four blocks: P, Q, R, and S. Block P is heavier than block Q but lighter than block R. Block Q is lighter than block R but heavier than block S. Which block is the heaviest?

 Think

Draw diagrams to show these relationships.

 Solve

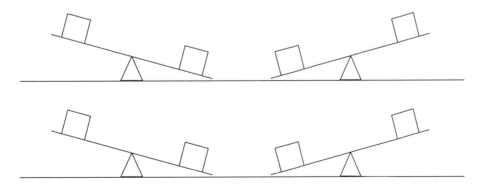

⭐ **Answer** **Block _____** is the heaviest.

(Answer: R)

Practice: Draw a Diagram

1. Pablo, Thad, and Jeremy are classmates. Jeremy is taller than Thad but shorter than Pablo. Who is the tallest?

💡 **Think**

✏️ **Solve**

⭐ **Answer**

2. Some children are in a line for ice cream. Sierra is the fourth child from the front and the fifth child from the end of the line. How many children are in the line?

💡 **Think**

✏️ **Solve**

⭐ **Answer**

3. There are 3 bags of rice. Bag X is lighter than bag Y. Bag Z is heavier than bag Y. Arrange the 3 bags of rice according to their weights, beginning with the lightest.

💡 **Think**

✏️ **Solve**

⭐ **Answer**

4. There are 4 students in a group. Carrie is younger than Delia but older than Alexa. Beth is older than Alexa but younger than Carrie. Who is the youngest in the group?

💡 **Think**

✏️ **Solve**

⭐ **Answer**

5. There are 3 different shapes: square, circle, and triangle. The square is bigger than the circle but smaller than the triangle. Draw the three shapes as a single diagram.

💡 **Think**

✏️ **Solve**

⭐ **Answer**

6. Ahmad, Brady, Caden, and Darius took part in a race. Ahmad finished after Brady and Caden. Brady finished before Caden and Darius. Caden finished after Darius but before Ahmad. Arrange the boys according to their positions, beginning with the first.

💡 **Think**

✏️ **Solve**

⭐ **Answer**

7. There are 5 ropes in a bag. Rope A is the longest. Rope B is longer than rope D but shorter than rope E. Rope C is longer than rope B but shorter than rope E. Arrange the 5 ropes according to their lengths, beginning with the shortest.

💡 **Think**

✏️ **Solve**

⭐ **Answer**

1. Julio has $12. His mother gives him $25. How much money does he have in all?

💡 **Think**

✏️ **Solve**

⭐ **Answer**

2. The picture graph below shows the number of children who like apples, pears, and oranges. How many children are there altogether?

 Think

☺		
☺	☺	
☺	☺	☺
☺	☺	☺
☺	☺	☺
apples	pears	oranges
Each ☺ stands for 1 child.		

Solve

⭐ **Answer**

3. Keisha has 8 pieces of red ribbon and 6 pieces of yellow ribbon. How many pieces of ribbon does she have altogether?

💡 **Think**

✏️ **Solve**

⭐ **Answer**

4. Mom buys 30 eggs. She uses 12 eggs to bake some cakes. How many eggs does she have left?

💡 **Think**

✏️ **Solve**

⭐ **Answer**

5. Liza takes 4 pencils and some pens from a box. She takes 6 more pens than pencils. How many pens does Liza take?

💡 **Think**

✏️ **Solve**

⭐ **Answer**

6. Tim has 20 marbles. His brother, Jim, has 5 fewer marbles than Tim. How many marbles does Jim have?

💡 **Think**

✏️ **Solve**

⭐ **Answer**

7. A group of 5 children need to shake hands once with each other. How many handshakes are exchanged altogether?

💡 **Think**

✏️ **Solve**

⭐ **Answer**

8. Mrs. Lang wants to make some sandwiches. She has 2 types of bread: white bread and whole-grain bread. She has 3 types of spread: tuna, egg salad, and peanut butter. How many types of sandwiches can she make?

💡 **Think**

✏️ **Solve**

⭐ **Answer**

9. Mrs. Shaw has 3 children. Sam is taller than Lily but shorter than Mason. Which of Mrs. Shaw's children is the tallest?

💡 **Think**

✏️ **Solve**

⭐ **Answer**

10. Susan is in line to buy a drink. She is the sixth person from the front and the second person from the end of the line. How many people are in the line?

💡 **Think**

✏️ **Solve**

⭐ **Answer**

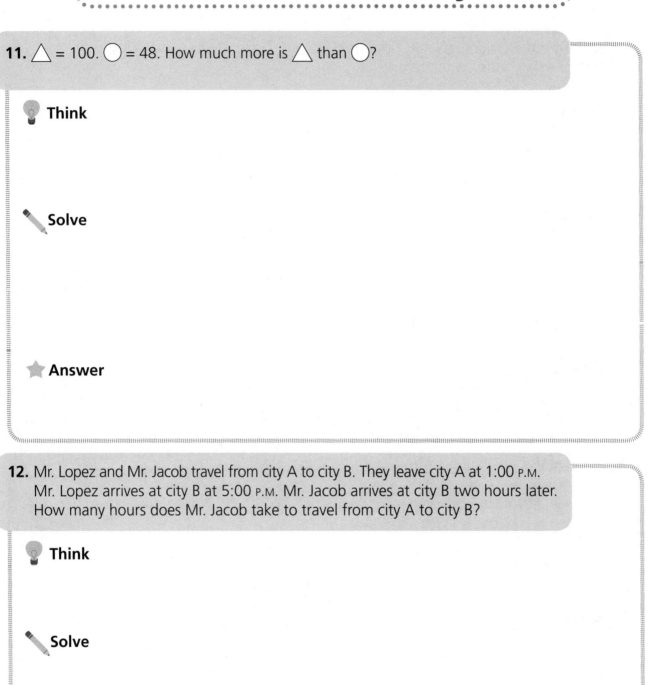

11. △ = 100. ○ = 48. How much more is △ than ○?

💡 **Think**

✏️ **Solve**

⭐ **Answer**

12. Mr. Lopez and Mr. Jacob travel from city A to city B. They leave city A at 1:00 P.M. Mr. Lopez arrives at city B at 5:00 P.M. Mr. Jacob arrives at city B two hours later. How many hours does Mr. Jacob take to travel from city A to city B?

💡 **Think**

✏️ **Solve**

⭐ **Answer**

13. Lamar is in a line. He is the fourth person from the front and the third person from the end of the line. How many people are in the line after the first person leaves the line?

 Think

 Solve

⭐ **Answer**

14. Jason has 4 coins: a 50-cent coin, a 25-cent coin, a 10-cent coin, and a 5-cent coin. How many different combinations can he make with any 2 coins?

💡 **Think**

✏️ **Solve**

⭐ **Answer**

15. How many rectangles are in the diagram?

💡 **Think**

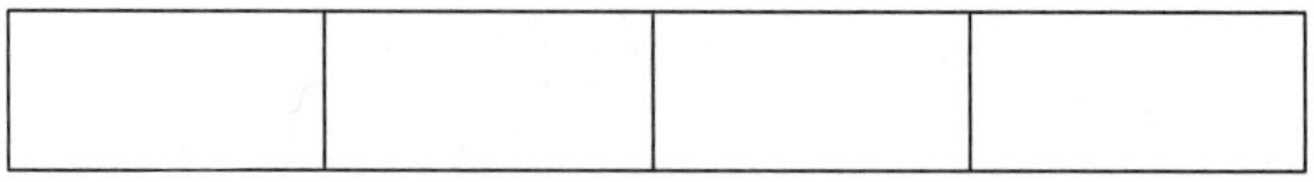

✏️ **Solve**

⭐ **Answer**

16. There are 18 hamsters at a pet shop. If 9 of them are sold, how many hamsters are left at the pet shop?

💡 **Think**

✏️ **Solve**

⭐ **Answer**

17. Riley watches 4 movies in January, 7 movies in February, and 3 movies in March. How many movies does Riley watch altogether?

💡 **Think**

✏️ **Solve**

⭐ **Answer**

18. Julie has 6 jelly beans. Her sister has 5 more jelly beans than Julie has. How many jelly beans does Julie's sister have?

 Think

 Solve

⭐ **Answer**

19. Three brothers, Austin, Blake, and Chase, are sitting on a bench. In how many different ways can they be seated on the bench?

💡 **Think**

✏️ **Solve**

⭐ **Answer**

20. Four friends go to a diner. There are 2 empty tables. Each table can seat 2 people. In how many ways can the friends be seated?

💡 **Think**

✏️ **Solve**

⭐ **Answer**

Mixed Practice: Intermediate

1. A seamstress has 4 pieces of cloth. Cloth A is longer than cloth B but shorter than cloth D. Cloth C is the shortest. Arrange the 4 pieces of cloth according to their lengths, beginning with the longest.

 Think

 Solve

⭐ **Answer**

38

© Singapore Asia Publishers Pte Ltd • FS-704114

2. The graph below shows how some students travel to school.
Read the clues:
Three students walk to school.
Twice as many students take the school bus as those who walk.
Two fewer students take the public bus than the school bus.
None travel to school by car.

Complete the graph by drawing the correct number of squares for each column.

💡 **Think**

✏️ **Solve**

⭐ **Answer**

public bus	walk	car	school bus
Each ☐ stands for 1 student.			

3. Danielle goes to a hobby shop. She buys 10 red beads, 15 blue beads, and 21 yellow beads. How many beads does she buy altogether?

💡 **Think**

✏️ **Solve**

⭐ **Answer**

4. In a parking lot, there are 12 small cars and 16 large cars. After an hour, 8 cars drive off. How many cars are left?

💡 **Think**

✏️ **Solve**

⭐ **Answer**

5. Aidan has 10 marbles. Taylor has 2 more marbles than Aidan. Rashad has 4 more marbles than Taylor. How many marbles does Rashad have?

💡 **Think**

✏️ **Solve**

⭐ **Answer**

6. Samia bakes 24 cakes. Her mother bakes 2 more cakes than Samia but 4 fewer than Samia's grandmother. How many cakes does Samia's grandmother bake?

💡 **Think**

✏️ **Solve**

⭐ **Answer**

Mixed Practice: Intermediate

7. Jimmy has 3 shirts: white, black, and yellow. He has 3 pairs of pants: white, black, and brown. In how many ways can he match a shirt to a pair of pants?

Think

Solve

Answer

8. How many triangles are in the diagram?

Think

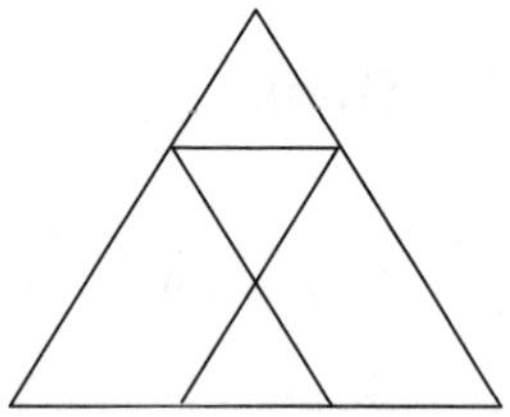

Solve

Answer

9. Tyler, Sage, Paul, and Meghan are in the same class. Sage is the tallest. Tyler is taller than Paul but shorter than Meghan. Arrange the children according to their heights, beginning with the shortest.

 Think

 Solve

⭐ **Answer**

10. Shade the pieces below that form the figure.

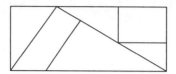

💡 **Think**

✏️ **Solve**

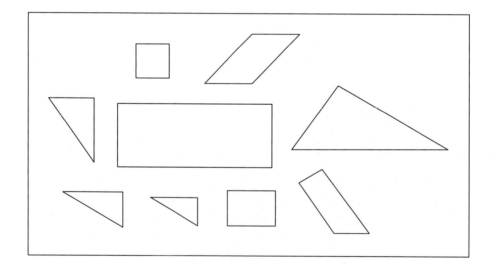

11. Javon buys some shrimp that have a total weight of 20 units. Sara buys some shrimp that weigh 5 units less than Javon's. Hannah buys some shrimp that weigh 8 units more than Sara's. Who buys the greatest weight of shrimp?

 Think

Solve

⭐ **Answer**

12. Antonio has 6 marbles. His brother has 3 times as many marbles as Antonio. How many marbles does Antonio's brother have?

💡 **Think**

✏️ **Solve**

⭐ **Answer**

13. Dante and his father are in line at a taxi stand. There are 5 people in front of them. There are 6 people behind them. How many people are left at the taxi stand after 3 of the people leave in a taxi?

 Think

✏️ **Solve**

⭐ **Answer**

14. Jack spends $25 on a book. He spends $18 more on a dictionary than on the book. How much does he spend in all?

 Think

 Solve

⭐ **Answer**

15. Lily has $40. After buying 4 pens, she has $24 left. How much does each pen cost?

💡 **Think**

✏️ **Solve**

⭐ **Answer**

Mixed Practice: Challenging

1. A farmer has 48 cows. He sells 12 cows to another farmer. He buys another 26 cows. How many cows does the farmer have in the end?

💡 **Think**

✏️ **Solve**

⭐ **Answer**

2. The figure below is made up of 12 toothpicks. Rearrange 2 toothpicks to form 7 squares.

💡 **Think**

✏️ **Solve**

⭐ **Answer**

3. Shane and his friend share $100. Shane gets $40 more than his friend. How much does each of them get?

 Think

 Solve

⭐ **Answer**

4. ☆ = 40

☆ = ❋ + ✲

❋ = 20 more than ✲

What is ✲?

 Think

 Solve

⭐ **Answer**

5. Every day Ms. Lee starts work at 9:00 in the morning. She has a lunch break of 1 hour. In the evening, she leaves at 6:00. How many hours does she work every day?

 Think

✏️ **Solve**

⭐ **Answer**

6.

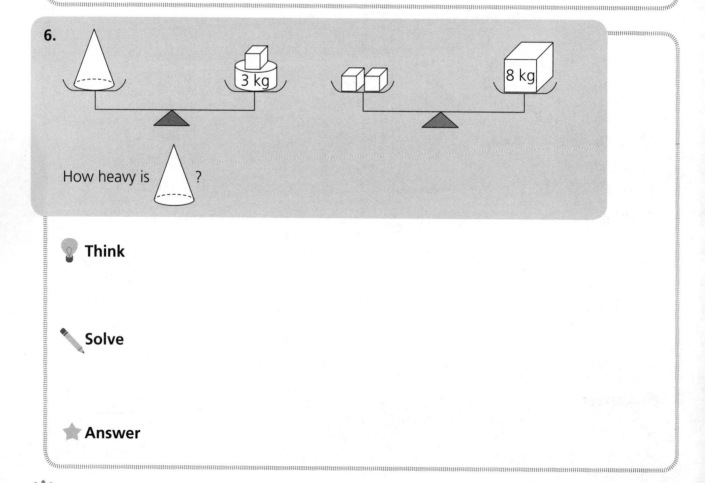

How heavy is 🔺 ?

 Think

✏️ **Solve**

⭐ **Answer**

Mixed Practice: Challenging

The graph below will show the number of stamps collected by 4 girls over two months, January and February. Use the graph to answer questions 7, 8, and 9.

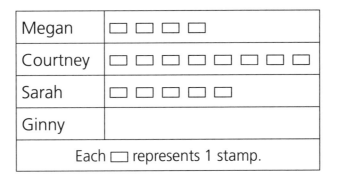

Megan	☐ ☐ ☐ ☐
Courtney	☐ ☐ ☐ ☐ ☐ ☐ ☐ ☐
Sarah	☐ ☐ ☐ ☐ ☐
Ginny	
Each ☐ represents 1 stamp.	

7. Ginny collects twice as many stamps as Sarah. Draw the correct number of rectangles for Ginny.

 Think

✏️ **Solve**

⭐ **Answer**

8. Courtney collects 2 more stamps in January than in February. How many stamps does she collect in February?

💡 **Think**

✏️ **Solve**

⭐ **Answer**

9. How many stamps do the 4 girls have altogether?

💡 **Think**

✏️ **Solve**

⭐ **Answer**

10. Arrange the children according to their heights, beginning with the shortest.

Ty   Sean   Ross   Sierra

 Think

 Solve

 Answer

11. Mrs. Foster bakes 50 cookies. She gives 28 cookies to her neighbor. She bakes another 24 cookies. How many cookies does Mrs. Foster have in the end?

 Think

 Solve

 Answer

12. Michael swam 10 laps in a swimming pool on Monday. He swam 11 laps on Tuesday, 12 laps on Wednesday, and 9 laps on Thursday. How many laps did Michael swim altogether?

 Think

Solve

Answer

13. There are 3 game booths at a fair. Booth A has 20 visitors. Booth B has 4 fewer visitors than booth A. Booth C has 8 more visitors than booth B. How many visitors does booth C have?

 Think

 Solve

⭐ **Answer**

14. Diners at a restaurant can choose from 2 main courses and 4 side dishes. If one meal is made up of 1 main course and 2 side dishes, how many different combinations of meals are there?

 Think

✏️ **Solve**

⭐ **Answer**

Mixed Practice: Challenging

15. How many squares are in the diagram?

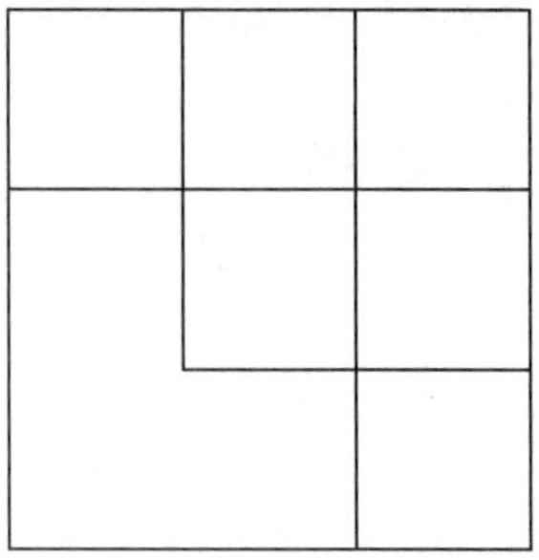

💡 **Think**

✏️ **Solve**

⭐ **Answer**

16. Five children take part in a quiz. Amber scores higher than Evan but lower than Dawn. Brandon scores higher than Cole but lower than Evan. Cole has the lowest score. Arrange the 5 children according to their scores, beginning with the highest.

💡 **Think**

✏️ **Solve**

⭐ **Answer**

Answer Key

Analyzing Parts and Wholes

pages 6–10

1.

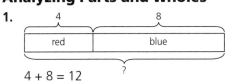

4 + 8 = 12
She has **12 beads** altogether.

2.

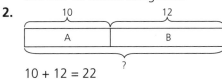

10 + 12 = 22
There are **22 cars** altogether.

3.

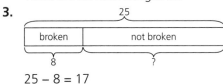

25 − 8 = 17
17 eggs are not broken.

4.

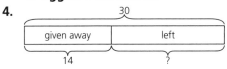

30 − 14 = 16
She has **16 stickers** left.

5.

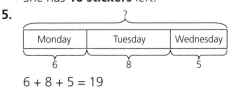

6 + 8 + 5 = 19
He reads **19 pages** altogether.

Comparing

pages 11–15

1.

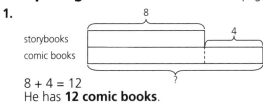

8 + 4 = 12
He has **12 comic books**.

2.

10 + 8 = 18
She buys **18 carnations**.

3.

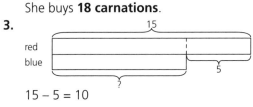

15 − 5 = 10

Ronald takes **10 blue balls**.

4.

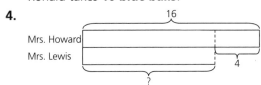

16 − 4 = 12
Mrs. Lewis sells **12 toasters**.

5.

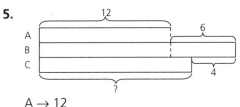

A → 12
B → 12 + 6 = 18
C → 18 − 4 = 14

There are **14 cupcakes** on tray C.

Act It Out

pages 16–20

1. 3 boys → A, B, C

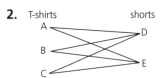

A + B, B + C, A + C
The coach can select **3 different pairs** of leaders.

2. T-shirts   shorts

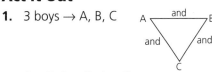

A + D, A + E, B + D, B + E, C + D, C + E
He can pair them in **6 ways**.

3. shoes   socks

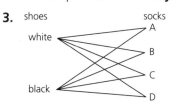

white + A, white + B, white + C, white + D,
black + A, black + B, black + C, black + D
She can pair them in **8 ways**.

4.

(Accept other correct answers.)

5.

(Accept other correct answers.)

Draw a Diagram

pages 21–25

1.

Jeremy   Thad   Pablo

Pablo is the tallest.

2.

front   end

Sierra

?

There are **8 children** in the line.

3.

X, **Y**, **Z**

4.

Carrie
Alexa
Delia
Beth

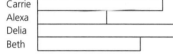

Alexa is the youngest in the group.

5.

6.

4th   3rd   2nd   1st
Ahmad   Caden   Darius   Brady

START   FINISH

Brady, **Darius**, **Caden**, **Ahmad**

7.

A
B
C
D
E

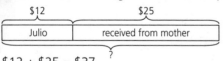

D, **B**, **C**, **E**, **A**

Mixed Practice: Easy

pages 26–37

1.

$12 $25

Julio	received from mother

?

$12 + $25 = $37
He has **$37** in all.

2. apples → 5
pears → 4
oranges → 3
5 + 4 + 3 = 12
There are **12 children** altogether.

3.

8   6

red	yellow

?

8 + 6 = 14
She has **14 pieces of ribbon** altogether.

4.

30

used	left

12   ?

30 − 12 = 18
She has **18 eggs** left.

5.

pencils
pens

4   6

?

4 + 6 = 10
Liza takes **10 pens**.

6.

20

Tim
Jim

5

?

20 − 5 = 15
Jim has **15 marbles**.

7. 5 children → A, B, C, D, E

From A → 4 handshakes (AB, AC, AD, AE)
From B → 3 handshakes (BC, BD, BE); Do not count
handshake with A again.
From C → 2 handshakes (CD, CE); Do not count
handshakes with A and B again.
From D → 1 handshake (DE); Do not count
handshakes with A, B, and C again.
4 + 3 + 2 + 1 = 10
10 handshakes are exchanged altogether.

8.

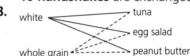

white   tuna
          egg salad
whole grain   peanut butter

white + tuna, white + egg salad, white + peanut
butter, whole grain + tuna, whole grain + egg salad,
whole grain + peanut butter
She can make **6 types** of sandwiches.

9.

Lily   Sam   Mason

Mason is the tallest.

10.

2nd
6th

front   end

Susan
?

7 people are in the line.

11.

48

○
△

?   100

100 − 48 = 52
△ is **52** more than ○.

12.

4 hours

Mr. Lopez
Mr. Jacob

1:00   5:00   2 hours

?

4 + 2 = 6
Mr. Jacob takes **6 hours**.

13.

There are **5 people** in the line.

14. 50¢ + 25¢, 50¢ + 10¢, 50¢ + 5¢,
25¢ + 10¢, 25¢ + 5¢,
10¢ + 5¢

He can make **6 different combinations**.

15.

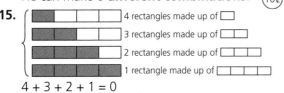

4 rectangles made up of ☐
3 rectangles made up of ☐☐
2 rectangles made up of ☐☐☐
1 rectangle made up of ☐☐☐☐

$4 + 3 + 2 + 1 = 0$
There are **10 rectangles**.

16.

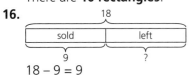

$18 - 9 = 9$
There are **9 hamsters** left at the pet shop.

17.

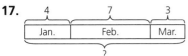

$4 + 7 + 3 = 14$
Riley watches **14 movies** altogether.

18.

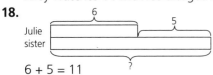

$6 + 5 = 11$
Her sister has **11 jelly beans**.

19. A, B, C   A, C, B
B, A, C   B, C, A
C, A, B   C, B, A

They can be seated on the bench in **6 different ways**.

20.

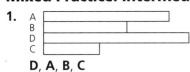

$1+2\rightarrow$A | $1+3\rightarrow$A | $1+4\rightarrow$A | $2+3\rightarrow$A | $2+4\rightarrow$A | $3+4\rightarrow$A
$3+4\rightarrow$B | $2+4\rightarrow$B | $2+3\rightarrow$B | $1+4\rightarrow$B | $1+3\rightarrow$B | $1+2\rightarrow$B

They can be seated at the tables in **6 different ways**.

Mixed Practice: Intermediate   pages 38–49

1.

D, A, B, C

2. walk $\rightarrow$ 3
school bus $\rightarrow$ 3 + 3 = 6
public bus $\rightarrow$ 6 – 2 = 4
car $\rightarrow$ 0

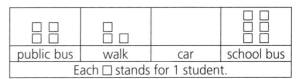

public bus	walk	car	school bus
Each ☐ stands for 1 student.			

3.

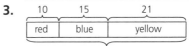

$10 + 15 + 21 = 46$
She buys **46 beads** altogether.

4.

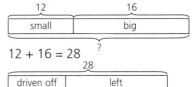

$12 + 16 = 28$

$28 - 8 = 20$
20 cars are left.

5.

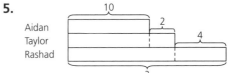

Taylor $\rightarrow 10 + 2 = 12$
Rashad $\rightarrow 12 + 4 = 16$
Rashad has **16 marbles**.

6.

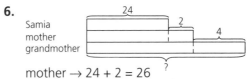

mother $\rightarrow 24 + 2 = 26$
grandmother $\rightarrow 26 + 4 = 30$
Samia's grandmother bakes **30 cakes**.

7. shirts   pants
white   white

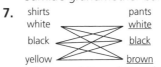

black   black

yellow   brown

white + white, white + black, white + brown,
black + white, black + black, black + brown,
yellow + white, yellow + black, yellow + brown
He can match them in **9 ways**.

8.

3   1   1   1
There are **6 triangles**.

9.

Sage   Tyler   Paul   Meghan

Paul, Tyler, Meghan, Sage

10.

11.

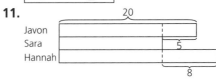

Sara → 20 − 5 = 15
Hannah → 15 + 8 = 23
Hannah buys the greatest weight of shrimp.

12.

6 + 6 + 6 = 18
His brother has **18 marbles**.

13.
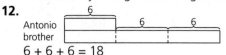
front of line
leave
back of line
Dante and his father
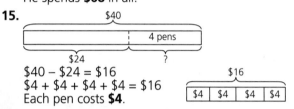
5   ?   6
10 people are left at the taxi stand.

14.
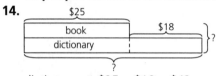
dictionary → $25 + $18 = $43
$43 + $25 = $68
He spends **$68** in all.

15.
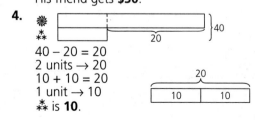
$40 − $24 = $16
$4 + $4 + $4 + $4 = $16
Each pen costs **$4**.

Mixed Practice: Challenging   pages 50–60

1.
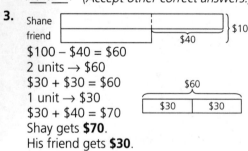
remaining → 48 − 12 = 36
36 + 26 = 62
The farmer has **62 cows** in the end.

2.
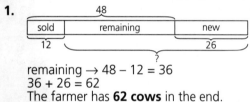
(Accept other correct answers.)

3.
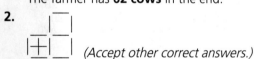
$100 − $40 = $60
2 units → $60
$30 + $30 = $60
1 unit → $30
$30 + $40 = $70
Shay gets **$70**.
His friend gets **$30**.

4.
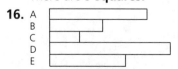
40 − 20 = 20
2 units → 20
10 + 10 = 20
1 unit → 10
✳✳ is **10**.

5.
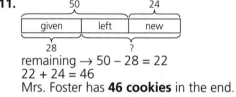
9:00   12:00   6:00
9 hours
9 − 1 = 8
She works **8 hours** every day.

6.
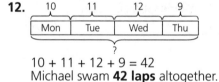
→ 8 kg   → 4 kg
→ 4 kg + 3 kg = 7 kg
is **7 kg**.

7. 5 + 5 = 10
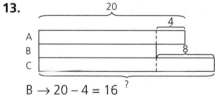

8.
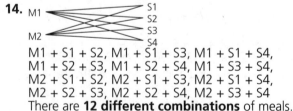
Jan   2   } 8
Feb
8 − 2 = 6
2 units → 6
3 + 3 = 6
1 unit → 3
She collects **3 stamps** in February.

9.
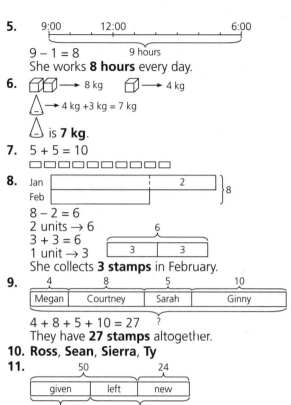
4   8   5   10
| Megan | Courtney | Sarah | Ginny |
4 + 8 + 5 + 10 = 27   ?
They have **27 stamps** altogether.

10. **Ross, Sean, Sierra, Ty**

11.
50   24
| given | left | new |
28   ?
remaining → 50 − 28 = 22
22 + 24 = 46
Mrs. Foster has **46 cookies** in the end.

12.
10   11   12   9
| Mon | Tue | Wed | Thu |
?
10 + 11 + 12 + 9 = 42
Michael swam **42 laps** altogether.

13.
20
4
A
B   8
C
?
B → 20 − 4 = 16
C → 16 + 8 = 24
Booth C has **24 visitors**.

14.
M1   S1
          S2
          S3
M2   S4
M1 + S1 + S2, M1 + S1 + S3, M1 + S1 + S4,
M1 + S2 + S3, M1 + S2 + S4, M1 + S3 + S4,
M2 + S1 + S2, M2 + S1 + S3, M2 + S1 + S4,
M2 + S2 + S3, M2 + S2 + S4, M2 + S3 + S4
There are **12 different combinations** of meals.

15.
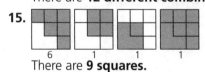
6   1   1   1
There are **9 squares**.

16.
A
B
C
D
E
Dawn, Amber, Evan, Brandon, Cole